Tips For Starting A Successful Flower Farm Business

Seraphina L. Parker

Introduction

Embarking on the journey of starting a successful flower farm business requires a blend of passion, strategic thinking, and practical know-how. This guide offers you a roadmap to turn your dream into a thriving reality, offering insights that span from self-awareness to arranging and selling your blossoms.

Self-awareness is your cornerstone. Before plunging into the flower farming world, ask yourself the hard questions. What's driving you to start this venture? How much time and money are you willing to invest? Understand your strengths, weaknesses, and your financial goals. This self-reflection sets the foundation for your flower farming journey.

Your ideal market is your compass. Dive into market research – understand consumer preferences, trends, and your potential competitors. Unearth common selling avenues for farmers, exploring options that align with your vision and goals. Your market understanding is the bedrock of your business strategy.

Introduction

Embarking on the journey of starting a successful flower farm business requires a blend of passion, strategic thinking, and practical know-how. This guide offers you a roadmap to turn your dream into a thriving reality, offering insights that span from self-awareness to arranging and selling your blossoms.

Self-awareness is your cornerstone. Before plunging into the flower farming world, ask yourself the hard questions. What's driving you to start this venture? How much time and money are you willing to invest? Understand your strengths, weaknesses, and your financial goals. This self-reflection sets the foundation for your flower farming journey.

Your ideal market is your compass. Dive into market research – understand consumer preferences, trends, and your potential competitors. Unearth common selling avenues for farmers, exploring options that align with your vision and goals. Your market understanding is the bedrock of your business strategy.

Launching your business requires careful planning. Your farm's name is your identity, and registering it as a business is your legal step forward. Insurance becomes your safety net, ensuring your business is shielded from uncertainties. Establishing a strong social media presence and a captivating website is your digital storefront, attracting customers to your blossoms.

The heart of your flower farm lies in where you grow. Delve into understanding the ideal characteristics of your growing field. Learn the art of cultivation, mastering bed spacing, orientation, and the nuances of wind and water. This foundation is essential for nurturing healthy blooms.

Deciding what to grow is a pivotal decision. Selecting the right flower varieties for your first year shapes your offerings and your business reputation. Following a planting guide is your roadmap to successful cultivation. Whether you're starting from seeds, cuttings, or direct sowing, each method demands careful attention.

As your blooms grow, so does your responsibility. This guide offers insights into fertilizing, managing diseases, and handling pests and animals. Keeping your flowers fresh from the moment of harvest is vital. Equip yourself with the right tools and solutions to preserve their beauty and allure.

Turning your flowers into profit requires a keen eye for arranging and selling. Learn the art of arranging, turning your blooms into captivating creations. Understand pricing strategies that balance profitability and customer appeal. Leverage social media, your website, and various avenues to reach your audience.

Starting a flower farm business is a dynamic journey, and this guide is your compass. From understanding your motivations to cultivating, harvesting, and arranging, every step is a vital piece of the puzzle. So, embark on this path with the knowledge that your passion and dedication can turn your flower farm dream into a blossoming reality.

Contents

KNOW YOURSELF

Flower farmers wear many hats: owner, manager, marketer, grower, harvester and arranger. In business terms that means you are now a CEO, CFO, farmer and florist. Each of these roles will be enhanced by who you are as a person; your unique giftings and abilities will shine through everything you do.

That's why it is so important that before you even plant a seed, you spend some time digging in and figuring out what exactly it is you, as an individual, have to offer your customers beyond flowers.

I know, I know.

You are probably sitting there thinking, what the hey? Why are we talking about personalities? Isn't this a book about growing and selling flowers?

Yes it is, and selling is exactly why we are talking about your personality. Since you are not only the farmer and florist behind your flower farm, but also the chief financial officer and chief executive officer, everything you do in running your farm is reflective of your unique strengths and weaknesses. What I want to do is help you position your flower farm in a way that highlights all of your strengths and leverages them in a way that compensates for your weaknesses.

As an entrepreneur and business owner, your flower farm, can, and should be, designed in a way that works for you.

More than just your personality, your position in life also determines what kind of farm you start. If you're a mom with two toddlers, your farm will look vastly different than that of a single college grad taking over his parents' farm.

There are five ways you, your personality, and your position in life affect your flower farming job:

1. Why you are starting a flower farm
2. How much money and time you have
3. How much money you need to make
4. Your strengths, passions, and beliefs
5. Your weaknesses

I want you to get real here and think about specific areas, both general and farming specific, where you excel and where you struggle, as well as what resources you have a lot of and where you are lacking. Be honest with yourself; by doing so you'll be able to start a farm that is designed just for you.

Still not sure what I'm talking about? Here's an example: do you hate chit chat? Then the local farmer's market may not be the place for you, but selling to florists could be the perfect fit.

For me, I'm amazeballs at seed starting. I have spreadsheets and lists galore. My calendar is planned to a T with all of the succession planting. But transplanting? No thank you. I'd rather get a root canal than plant out those thousands of baby plants. So how do I use this information to my advantage?

I plan transplanting parties with my friends. I give them flowers and seedlings in exchange for a couple hours of help out in the field. I use my strengths (seed starting and planning) to account for my weaknesses.

Be true to yourself and design a farm that works for you.

1. Why are you starting a flower farm?

Think of yourself like a tree: your why, your reasoning for starting a flower farm, is your roots. It needs to be deep and founded. Your why is what will keep you strong when the winds start blowing.

It's okay if one of your whys is additional income, you know I'm all about making money farming. But money isn't the kind of why I'm talking about here.

The kind of why that will keep you keepin' on when you have a crop failure or thrips infestation is deeper than that. It's about what you want to accomplish with your flower farm, it's how you want to serve your customers, it's emotional and raw.

Your why needs to be raw and emotional because we are coming in on a huge trend in marketing that is reflective of our grandparents' generation. Your customers want more than just flowers, they want a connection with you, the whole package. They want to do business with a real, honest-to-goodness person, just like yourself.

In his book *Start With Why*, Simon Sinek defines how important knowing your why is.

"Very few people or companies can clearly articulate WHY they do WHAT they do. By WHY I mean your purpose, cause or belief - WHY does your company exist? WHY do you get out of bed every morning? And WHY should anyone care?

People don't buy WHAT you do, they buy WHY you do it.

We are drawn to leaders and organizations that are good at communicating what they believe. Their ability to make us feel like we belong, to make us feel special, safe and not alone is part of what gives them the ability to inspire us."

Your customers want to be inspired. They want to belong. And they want to buy from you for more than superficial reasons. So take your time defining your why. Journal or type it out. Keep it posted somewhere in your house so you can remember your reasoning and bring it into your everyday business to-do's.

2. How much money and time do you want to invest in farming?

Ugh, I hate talking about money. You too? The cold, hard reality is it needs to factor into your plans. You already know this; how much you have to invest will impact how much money you make. So think of an ideal number in your head of how much you have to invest at the moment. Got it? Awesome. Now double it. That's most likely how much you will end up spending.

Farming expenses are often hidden. They pop up when you least expect them. If you are cautious and like to be on the safe side, think about spending only half of your allotted funds from the beginning so you can always have a safety net.

Investing in your flower farm, however, is more than money, it is also time and land. Take stock of your money, time and land as you plan out your farm.

3. How much money do you need to make?

Flowers are a high value crop for the amount of space required. Consider a row of sunflowers, 3 ft wide by 50 ft long, if you plant them intensively every 6" (square foot gardening style!) and sell them for $1 each, then that is $4 for every 1 sq ft of space. Or, $600 for the whole row. Pretty great, right?

However, flowers are a very time intensive crop. From planting to netting to harvesting to storing, each and every dollar is well earned. Not to mention losses in the field due to wind, pests and animals. Seeds are cheap, your time is not.

Be (very) general here when calculating how much time it will take you to work on your flower farm. After a month or two you will have a good sense of how much time you are spending and how much you need to charge for your flowers in order to pay yourself.

Every new business takes time to become profitable. Keep that in mind when you get discouraged and feel like you are butting up against a brick wall. Flower farming is time and labor intensive, it takes a while to build a customer base and there are lots of benefits to this job outside of money. If you are smart about building your business you will become profitable.

4. What are your strengths, passions, and beliefs?

On a practical level, your strengths help determine your flower farming plan. Are you good at record keeping? Personal relations? Flower arranging?

If you struggle knowing your own skills, ask yourself, what do I like to do? Or, what do I *think* I will like most about growing flowers?

Defining these will help you evaluate your farm goals.

On an inspirational level, your strengths and passions are closely related to your why. Your customers want more than pretty flowers, they want to feel connected to you and to know what unique things you bring to the table for them.

This can be tricky to determine. For me it has taken a lot of soul searching and deep reflection to really understand what this looks like for myself and my business. Want to hear it? Here ya go:

I believe in connecting with people and inspiring them to find beauty in the everyday.

Short, sweet, and to the point.   What are your unique strengths? And how do you want to convey them to your customers?

5. What are your weaknesses?

Figuring out what you are bad at is just as important as recognizing your strengths! Knowing where you struggle gives you the ability to shift your focus and ask for help in those areas. Don't discount physical weaknesses too.

Once you've defined your weaknesses, think about how you can compensate for them. Find a way to leverage your strengths against your weaknesses.

The time you spend getting to know yourself better will pay off in the long run, friend!

―――

Big Ideas:

- People buy your WHY, not your What
- Plan your farm around your strengths
- Learn how to compensate for your weaknesses
- Decide how much time, money and land you are willing to invest in your farm

―――

Get Real: Time to Dig In

1. Why are you starting a flower farm?

2. How did you first get the idea to grow and sell cut flowers?

3. Who is your flower farming inspiration?

4. From your perspective, how does flower farming differ from flower gardening?

5. Why do you want to start a flower farm? List three big picture reasons (they need to be more than monetary).

6. What are your strengths as they pertain to flowers? Are you good at seed starting? Designing?

7. Where do you struggle with flower farming? What aspects make you cringe? And what limitations do you have? A full time job? A baby or two?

8. What are your strengths as a business owner? How does your personality play into this? Are you personable or reserved? Is it easy for you to fill the customer service role? Or do you like to work behind the scenes?

9. What are your weaknesses as a business owner? Where do you lag behind? Record keeping? Etc…

10. What aspects of running a flower farming business can you really excel in due to your strengths? And where will you (or do you) struggle?

11. If you could pick one overarching theme for your flower farm, what would it be? This should be service based. What do want to give or do for your customers beyond providing flowers for them?

12. What is your why behind the above question? Why do you want to serve your customers in that way?

2

FIND YOUR IDEAL MARKET

HOW TO DETERMINE YOUR FLOWER FARMING NICHE

Flower farming is full of long hours, hard physical labor, and an (often) undervalued product. To make this business worth your time you will need to be successful in selling and marketing. Your success is largely dependent on the demand for your flowers and in order to figure out what that demand is, you have to develop an understanding of two primary things: who your customers are and when they buy flowers.

You might already have an idea of who your customer will be. I sure did when I started my first season. Y'all, I was going to sell to florists. Only florists. I wanted nothing to do with selling directly to consumers because I didn't like arranging. Florists need flowers and selling to them saves me loads of time designing and marketing. Win-win for this busy momma of two toddlers.

It worked perfectly for one whole month. Turns out summer can be S.L.O.W. in my area for florists. They didn't need my flowers.

Maybe you've found yourself in a similar position; a field full of flowers with nowhere for them to go. What do you do when your entire plan has to shift and change?

You find out what people really want.

Turns out, the people in my little town really wanted market style bouquets. I held a week of giveaways on Facebook, and my clientele started growing leaps and bounds. I sent flowers to the largest regional farmers market with some farmer friends who sold them for me. I also set up a roadside stand which often sold out.

You see, your ideal market isn't about you at all, it's about them: the people who will be buying and enjoying your flowers.

This is where marketing flowers gets a little tricky. You'll need to do some groundwork and start asking real live people some questions about what they want.

The flower industry is alive and well, I can guarantee you people are buying and selling flowers in your part of the world. Your job is to find those people and ask them how you can serve them better.

I want to help you plan out exactly what you are going to sell and how you are going to sell it based on who will be buying your flowers.

I know this is hard, and can be complicated, because how do you plan for your flower farm before you have flowers?

Ask questions. Really get to know who might buy flowers from you. Find out what they want, more than just flowers. Become their friend and confidant. And genuinely try to serve and help them. Make the process of buying from you as easy as possible.

Here are a few general questions to get you started thinking about your ideal market.

In the Get Real: Dig In section you'll find more specific questions to help guide you along this process of finding your ideal market. I've also included a link to a survey you can use to learn how to help and serve your customers.

General Market Questions

What is the current flower market like?

Are you in a community that values art and aesthetics? The culture of your immediate area will affect your business. Everyone loves flowers, but not everyone values them.

In my hometown and the surrounding area the going price for a bouquet of flowers is $5. Seriously. What is your area like?

Who is buying and selling flowers?

Here is where you get to really dig in and do some tangible research. Where do people buy flowers currently? Florists? Wholesalers? Farmers?

Google is your best friend here. Visit all of the farmer's markets within a two hour drive, look at directories (www.slowflowers.com, www.ascfg.org), go to different grocery stores to see what they offer. Do your homework here to get an idea of what others are selling.

What are the design styles and trends?

Is there a popular design or trend you can fill that other florists aren't providing?

I got into flower farming because I loved to grow, but my customers buy from me for my designs. One customer told me she loves my work because I don't do anything traditional. I am the only one in my immediate area who offers garden-style bouquets. This can be the perfect opportunity for you to set yourself apart by offering different floral arrangements from the competition.

8 Common Selling Avenues for Farmers

The following is a list of traditional ways flower farmers have sold flowers. It's a great place to start but don't be afraid to try new things! I've also included a list of the supplies you'll need for each category.

Farmer's Markets

When you first think of selling flowers, a farmer's market is probably what comes to mind. They can be a great source of income, or they can be a total fail. It really depends on your area. You can either make bank or go home with barely enough to cover your time spent, let alone the cost of the flowers you grow.

Contact your local markets and ask about their foot traffic. Who is selling flowers there already? What is popular and what isn't? Do they think the market could properly support a flower farm? You will need to do some research too. What is the economic and social status in your area? Do people value local and sustainable growers? *And more importantly, do they value it enough to shell out their own money?*

I am grateful to have established farming friends that take my flowers to market for me. Not all markets allow this, so be sure to check before you count on it as a source of income. Farmer's markets do offer a chance for your name to get out there and are a good opportunity to show off your flowers and design work. Overall, farmer's markets can be a great way to promote your farm.

What you'll need:

- A tent
- Display stand for your flowers.
- Farm and pricing signs
- Business cards

Retail Florists

What you want to do when it comes to florists is "wow" them. They can often be a bit skeptical of flower farmers, and for good reason. They need to know that you are a professional grower who can supply them on a consistent basis with quality product. A lot of growers will recommend waiting to approach florists until you have flowers to give them.

I was too impatient and couldn't wait, so I went ahead and introduced myself before my season. However, I still had to show them that I could actually grow flowers. While it helped to establish relationships with them early on, they needed to see my flowers to really understand what I was offering.

If florists are your ideal market, take time to find out exactly how you can help them.

Start by making a list of all local florists and then do some research. When you approach them you should have a list of what you are growing, when (approximately) it will be available, and how much money you are asking per bunch. Take the time to ask them what they recommend, and what they usually order, and what they wish they had access to but don't.

Talking to florists isn't as scary as it can seem, I promise. They are hard working entrepreneurs just like us who also understand the dichotomy between selling and creating. You got this! I know it can be hard because you want to help florists, not take business from them. Just be kind and friendly. Operate from a place of true service and I'm sure they'll love you too.

What you'll need:

- Price list
- Business cards

Grocery Stores

Selling to grocery stores requires a few more steps: you will need to be prepared to supply a stand for the flowers and bar codes for each bouquet. Typically grocery stores will take a 30-40% commission. Look for stores that are already buying product from local vegetable growers. They will be the most receptive to selling your flowers. You will want to give them numbers, how many bouquets you will be supplying for how many weeks and what they should do with any unsold bouquets.

What you'll need:

- Display stand
- Bar codes
- Sleeves or wraps
- CVBN tablets (https://www.chrysal.com/en-us/products/chrysal-cvbn)

CSA - Community Shared Agriculture

When you and your customers hear "CSA shares", the first thought that comes to mind is vegetables. A CSA works by the customer paying the farmer before the season begins for a weekly "share" of vegetables. It is giving the customer a guarantee of products on a weekly basis while ensuring you, the farmer, a way to get your product directly into the hands of your customers. The benefit of selling this way is that CSAs are paid upfront which provides some capital before the growing season starts.

This same concept can be applied to flower farms. You might want to try calling it something aside from a CSA; my customers got a little confused since I'm selling flowers, not vegetables. But they loved the idea of a weekly bouquet subscription.

What's nice about CSA's is that you get to decide exactly what you want to do and how you want to do it. You have the ability to chose when it starts and how long it will last. You can offer monthly, bi-monthly or weekly options. The length of your subscription is also up to you (10 weeks is fairly typical). You can do longer or shorter subscriptions depending on where you live and what you think your market will support.

Also, it's a great way to move product when you have excess. For instance, my CSA doesn't even start until July because that's when I have twice as many flowers.

What you'll need:

- Drop off site (or delivery plan)
- Detailed sales page on your website explaining exactly what you are offering
- Buckets/display stand

Businesses & Restaurants

Selling to businesses and restaurants is a great way to raise brand awareness while selling flowers. To make things simple for restaurants, you can offer to loan them vases each week along with the flowers.

I take flowers in bud vases to my local coffee shop, and each week I take home the dirty vases to wash. This adds value for local businesses, because it is one less thing for them to worry about. Approaching businesses after you have flowers is the best bet. Give them an arrangement or two, and they will realize how much beauty flowers bring to their space.

What you'll need:

- Vases
- Delivery system

Roadside Stand

My roadside stand is my bread and butter. I live in a small town in the middle of Iowa and it's amazeballs how many people stop by on a weekly basis!

Typically stands are left unattended. They seem to work best in public populated areas with a lot of traffic. Try offering two different price points.

I read about a stand on the Flower Farmer's Facebook group that makes $700 a week! They keep their stand stocked with $5 bouquets and sell them on a regular basis, because they are located by a country club and golf course. (I couldn't find the original post, but if this is you, send me an email, I think you're amazing!)

If you don't have a prime location, you can look into setting up a stand in town. Head to your city hall to find out what license they require.

We're in the middle of moving so I am having to reassess my stand. At the moment it is in our side lot right along one of two main throughways in our town. I've talked to one of the local coffee shop owners about putting it outside their store. It would be stocked with bouquets every weekend and to keep thefts to a minimum, I'd have a camera in place with a warning that anyone who steals will have their picture posted on the community Facebook page. I can't imagine a worse punishment!

What you'll need:

- License
- Stand
- Lock box
- Prominent location
- Signs

Weddings

Weddings and events can often be the most lucrative option for flower farmers. They command a higher price than market bouquets but also require more work and design technique. If you are interested in selling to brides, read this article that Lennie Larkin of B-Side Farm wrote titled, "How to Become a Farmer/Florist - My Talk at the Oregon Small Farms Conference."

It's chock full of helpful info and she lays out her step by step process of becoming a farmer/florist that caters to brides.

What you'll need:

- Detailed sales page on your website explaining your services
- Contract & sales proposal

PYO - Pick Your Own

This is another way to sell flowers that is largely dependent on your location. It is a great option especially for those in metropolitan areas - a place where not many people garden themselves and are looking for experiences in nature.

What you'll need:

- Cute signage
- Pricing list
- Business cards
- Buckets for customers
- Clippers for customers

You know all of the work you did in Chapter One defining your personal strengths and weaknesses? Use those notes along with the notes in this chapter to assess where you fit in. Take some time to think about what you want to do, and how you want to do it. Which selling avenues are best for your personality and strengths? Which aren't as good of an idea for you?

You can't be everything to everyone. And it's okay if your plans change! Flexibility and determination are both needed here. You will have successes and failures. Learn from your mistakes and use those lessons o guide your farm planning and goals.

Big Ideas:

- Focus on helping and serving your customers
- Do what works for you and your personal strengths
- Find areas that are lacking in the current flower industry and fill that need

Get Real: Time to Dig In

1. What is the current flower market like in your area?

2. Does your community generally value arts and beauty? Or are they fairly conservative in their spending?

3. What is the economic and social status of your area? Do people value local and sustainable growers? And more importantly, do they value local and sustainable enough to shell out their own money?

4. Where do people buy flowers currently? Florists? Wholesalers? Farmers?

5. Who are the other flower farmers in your area?

6. Where do other flower farms in your area sell their flowers? What are their primary sources of income? Market? Stands? Grocery stores?

7. Where are florists currently buying flowers?

8. Who are the florists within a reasonable delivery distance?

9. Who do your florists sell to? And what are their primary sources of income? Weddings? Mother's day? Graduation?

10. What do your florists struggle with? What needs do they have that aren't being met?

11. What are the design styles and trends in your community? Is there a popular design or trend you can fill that other florists aren't providing?

12. How do you think the strengths and weaknesses you identified in Section #1 can add value to your potential customers?

13. What is one thing that you are awesome at that isn't being done by other florists and flower farmers in your area?

3

STARTING YOUR BUSINESS

N ow that you have a better idea of where and how you are going to sell your flowers it's time to legalize it all and actually start a company.

Yep, it can be scary when you aren't sure if flower farming is something you want to commit your life too.

Still, as I'm sure you've learned by now, I wholeheartedly believe in starting your farm with your business in mind. To that end I want you to go into growing and selling flowers with as many facts and as much knowledge on selling as you have on growing. Because of this I think that every single person selling flowers needs to be fully licensed and insured.

It is tempting to think of yourself as just a small backyard farmer when you don't have hoop houses or heavy equipment, but even if that is the case you need to take the proper steps in running a business.

Proper licensing gives your customers the trust they need in order to purchase from you. It protects both you and them.

We are covering a lot in this chapter, everything from naming and registering your business, to using social media. So hang on and get ready to start your farm!

Naming Your Farm

Okay, now let's talk names!

Naming your business is fairly self-explanatory, but necessary for filing your business with your state.

It can be a little overwhelming trying to think of the right name so here are some ideas to help you brainstorm:

- Choose a name that clearly states what you are and/or what you do, UNLESS you are an event florist. If that's the case you can easily just use your own name like a lot of wedding photographers do.
- Google your name idea and see what else pops up. Your state will have a list of all the businesses registered so you can verify that yours is unique.
- Make a list of all the potentially unique factors about your location or your farm
- Check Instagram & Facebook to see if the name you want is available
- Ask friends and family for their advice!

Registering Your Farm as a Business

You can own and operate your flower farm in one of three categories:

1. Sole-proprietor
2. DBA: Doing Business A
3. LLC: Limited Liability Corporation

Which you chose is up to you. From a tax perspective, these are all treated the same. You will have to pay personal income taxes, quarterly estimates, and sales tax.

I am not an expert by any means, but I would recommend you start off on the right foot with an LLC, especially if you are concerned about your personal liability. An LLC, when operated correctly, will protect your personal assets from liability.

Speaking of liability, I have to add I am not a tax professional or a lawyer and everyone's situation is different. So get the advice of professionals to figure out what is best in your situation.

Insurance

Insurance is especially important if you have customers coming to your property to buy flowers. Contact your current insurance provider with questions. At the very least they will have the information you need or be able to point you in the right direction.

Questions to ask your insurance agent:

- Can you have farm visits?
- What steps do you need to take to protect yourself from potential harm to visitors?
- How large is the coverage policy?

Social Media Presence

The days of big impersonal businesses are on the way out. Social media is changing how we interact with each other and in essence changing the way we buy from each other.

We are starting to want personal connections with the people we buy from.

Social media is a key tool in selling flowers today. Not only that, your website and social media accounts need to look professional and be well designed. You are selling flowers, so essentially you are selling beauty itself and your web presence needs to reflect that.

Website

There are a couple different ways to go about making a website: you can hire a professional, or make one yourself. There are a lot of really great services that make building your own site easier. Squarespace and Wix are the two I use for my websites. I can't recommend 3 Cow Marketing's free website training videos, with Charlotte Smith, enough! They make it super duper easy with tutorials on setting up a Squarespace website. On top of that Charlotte has a lot of information on email marketing and how to automate your welcome email.

You can find the videos at
www.3cowmarketing.com/freetraining/.

Facebook Page

Facebook business pages are a great marketing tool. Because of how search engine optimization works, your Facebook page will often be what pops up in a Google search of your farm's name.

One word of caution here: you can't, and shouldn't, sell products through your Facebook page. Instead, you should redirect people to your website.

To set up a page, log in your personal account and go to the bottom left corner of your home screen. You'll see page listed under the "create" section. When you do create a page, make sure it is a business page and you have your address listed. Without an address Facebook won't let people give you reviews.

Once you have your page up and running share it with friends and in community groups.

Things to remember to have on your page:

- Address
- Website link
- Clear directions on where and how to buy flowers from you

Instagram

Instagram is the bomb dot com for beautiful images. It is also a great way to build relationships with your customers (and potential customers)! To that end, make sure you are posting more than just pictures of your pretty flowers. Your customers want to know the real you. They want to trust you and see what you have in common.

There are two questions you need to ask yourself every time you post:

1. Am I adding value to my customers by posting this?
2. Does this image align with the type of customer I want to attract?

I think too often we think of instagram as a way to either humble brag or document our day to day. Instead, take the time to be intentional with what you post. Think about it as a way to add value to your audience and showcase what you do:

- How can you inspire and encourage them today?
- What can you do to educate them?
- What do they find entertaining?
- Am I portraying my work well?

It is a great tool not only to promote your farm, but also to find other flower designers in your area. Use local hashtags to attract new followers. Look and see what other flower farmers are using. There's even a thread in the Flower Farmer's Facebook Group of hundreds of IG names that you could follow.

So as you go about planning your Instagram content keep these things in mind:

- Post about more than flowers
- Think about adding value to your customers
- Build community - by doing this you'll build your brand

The whole act of running a business is essentially one of building trust with people. When you operate legally, you are communicating you have nothing to hide.

The same thing is true of social media - when you share more of your life with people they will form a connection and want to support you.

Big Ideas:

- Legalize it
- Focus on adding value to your customers
- Use social media to connect with your customers

Get Real: Time to Dig In

1. Do you have a name picked out for your farm? List all of your ideas here:

2. Who is your current insurance provider? Do they cover home-based businesses as well?

3. Do you have a website set up already? Does it effectively communicate what it is you do and how you help people?

4. How are you going to connect with your customers? Facebook? Instagram? Email?

5. What topics do you feel comfortable sharing about online?

6. How can you serve, educate, entertain or inspire your customers?

7. What things can you explain to or show your customers to help them trust you?

4

WHERE TO GROW

inding the right location for your flower field is kind of like playing a game of Russian roulette with the elements. You can never be 100% sure on anything.

But despite this fact, it's still important to think carefully about where you are going to plant. You may not be able to control the elements, but there are a lot of other things you *can* control.

When picking a location, consider the following aspects of any given field:

- Water availability
- Soil quality
- Wind patterns
- Weed pressure
- Pest & animal pressure
- Distance from water hook ups and buildings
- Water run-off and pooling

You can lose crops to just about anything no matter how much care you take in choosing the right location. But the care you take in determining a good growing location will pay off in the end, both physically in terms of manual labor, and monetarily when you produce superior crops.

And don't forget to think about the   convenience of your field to water and tools. You will be hauling buckets of water for harvesting, hoses for watering, not to mention all the tools and bed prep you'll be doing. Proximity to water and tool storage are both factors that need consideration. Flower farming is tough work physically, so anything you can do to make it easier on yourself is an added bonus.

Ideal Field Characteristics

I know that life isn't ideal; a lot of us are farming on poor quality soil, or on the plains where the winds never seem to stop. And it's okay. You can grow windbreaks, or amend the soil. There are varieties of flowers that can better tolerate drought. With time and trial and error you'll figure it out. However, I will say you need to think twice about planting flowers on land that doesn't have adequate light, water and soil. If it's just not possible on your own land, you will need to lease or rent land where conditions are more favorable.

So what does the ideal plot look like?

- 6+ hours of sun each day
- Natural wind barrier
- Close to water source & flower storage/cooler
- No more than a 5% slope, preferably facing south
- Good drainage, no sitting water

The first thing you want to do when it comes to your field is get a soil test. Your local university extension office will be able to help you out here. If you are growing with organic methods, you will need to modify their suggestions. Order in bulk compost every year to amend your soil in addition to what the soil test shows. Landscape supply companies will often carry it, and you can expect to pay anywhere from $25-$50+ per yard of finished (sifted) compost.

How to Cultivate

Cultivating largely depends on the current condition of your plot and the equipment you have access to.

Fallow Hay Field

- Disc. Then till. Then till again. And maybe till again one more time for good measure. Disking is necessary to break the sod. (Ask me how I know, ha! I can even send you horror pictures of what a field looks like if you only till ….)

Current Garden Area

- Till. Then broadfork. If you have already been working the soil than you most likely have a good idea of what nutrients it will need.

Urban Lot

- Build raised beds or sheet mulch (compost). Amendments are doubly crucial if you are growing on a previous building spot.

There has been a huge shift in people's thinking about soil health. We as a society want to take care of the earth, and it's great.

Since we are in the middle of a move, I have a new field to prep and I would love to do only sheet mulching and occulation for all of my beds. I'm not sure how to do it on a large scale, but I'll keep you updated on my progress. (If you figure it out let me know!)

If you are looking for more information on no-till methods check out the book, *The Market Gardener* and Bare Mountain Farm's Website, www.baremountainfarm.com

Bed Spacing and Orientation

The general recommendations for bed width are either 4' or 3'. Beds 4' in width are more efficient but it can be more physically demanding to reach across such a large space. 3' foot beds are more manageable. It all comes down to how much space you have on your property. If you have the room for slightly narrower beds, that is a plus. Width between rows will depend largely on your plan for weed suppression. I am trying to maximize my production, so I have 4' wide beds covered in 6' wide landscape fabric which results in 1' extra on either side.

You will find growers with both north-south and east-west bed orientation. Don't spend too much time worrying about it. You can always try the opposite direction next year. However, if you plant an east-west row full of sunflowers (or other extra-tall cuts), the eastern ones will be shaded by the westernmost sunflowers in the afternoon.

Wind

Wind is another consideration when it comes to plot layout. Wind can do a lot of damage to flowers, causing them to not grow quite as tall or even flattening them. There are several different solutions, the best being a permanent (natural) wind fence made out of various trees or shrubs.

Temporary solutions include netting or artificial wind fencing. Hortonova netting is the only brand of netting I know of. You can order it online (even from Amazon!) and it works great. You'll need t-posts or PVC pipes with notches in them to use it along a row. If you Google how to use it you'll find lots of info.

Wind fences can also be made from burlap and 2x2s (uline), or you can plant fast growing rye to provide a temporary short season windbreak. For the long term, consider planting a natural windbreak around the perimeter of your plot to protect your plants.

Water

Oh water. I've already mentioned how I think watering is dumb. Seriously, I live in Iowa. It rains all the time. Except when it doesn't and then all of my plants die. So take this from me, even if you live in an area with a large amount of rainfall, you'll still need to water on a regular basis. Like a lot.

You'll want your field to be well draining and close to a water source. Plan on watering new transplants twice a day and watering established plants every other day.

Your watering options are:

Hand watering: this is a great option for the plants but not necessarily for you. You'll end up spending more time than you'd like with a hose.

Sprinkler system: this isn't as efficient as far as water usage goes, but is still a good option.

Drip tape: this is the most efficient in terms of both your time and water usage. Check out dripworks.com for videos and kits.

When planning your field location it pays off to spend more time cultivating the right plot. You'll have enough work on your hands, so don't let poor location choice drag you down too.

———

Big Ideas:

- Choose a plot based on ideal characteristics
- Take into account all potential issues including pests and weeds

---

Get Real: Time to Dig In

When deciding on a field ask yourself these questions:

1. How much sunlight does it get in any given day?

2. What was the land previously used for?

3. What is the soil fertility?

4. How is the drainage?

5. Where is the water access?

6. What about animals? Deer? Moles? Groundhogs?

7. What weeds will I be fighting?

8. How can I make my work easier with this particular field?

5

WHAT TO GROW

VARIETIES TO GROW AND MAKE A PROFIT FROM YOUR FIRST SEASON

When I first thought about starting a cut flower farm, the biggest question I agonized over was *what do I grow? What makes a good cut? What doesn't? Will this particular variety have a good vase life? What would work better?*

Inspiration for what to grow is everywhere. When I first started out I would spend days pouring over seed catalogs and drooling over certain varieties. Deciding what I actually wanted to grow, however, was an entirely different matter.

I would lie on my bed with all of my flower books open and make list after list of flowers to grow with notes about their particular needs. As I moved from one resource to another, I found myself adding things and then crossing them out as the recommendations changed from book to book. I felt like I was drowning in cut flower possibilities, and my head spun from all the beautiful varieties.

I found myself drawn the most to the unattainable flowers. Things like tree peonies and the David Austin roses that need years to produce enough to make a profit. How do I choose what to grow right now? What should I grow to be successful? To prove to myself that this was something I could do?

Sometimes flower farming can be a lot like advanced mathematics. If you've ever taken calculus, you know that distance is a function of time and space. Flowers are the same way. A lot more goes into a good cut flower than whether or not it can be cut.

As a flower farmer you need to consider every aspect that makes up each flower. Is it easy to grow? Low maintenance? Does it fill a certain design aesthetic? Is it readily available as seeds? Or plugs? How much space does it need? How cold hardy is it? How susceptible to disease is it? Do you have time to grow it between your last and first frost dates?

All of these things are important to consider. For instance, bachelor buttons are easily grown from seed, fairly cold hardy, readily available, can be in demand from florists, have a unique shade of blue, but they are a pain to harvest so many people don't grow them. See what I mean? It is so important to consider more than the particular design aesthetic of flowers.

And friends, take this from someone who has grown all the wrong flowers for the wrong reasons: if you want to make money selling flowers you have to pick flowers that you can sell. They need to be:

- In demand
- Not (overly) fussy or needy
- Fairly disease resistant
- Have a long vase life

Sounds super boring, doesn't it? If you are anything like me and can't seem to keep your wits about you when confronted with ALL the pretty flower varieties, I can help. That's why I wrote this chapter.

This is a list of flowers you can grow and profit from in one year. To get it all in a spreadsheet go here: growflowers.org/freestuff.

Some of these varieties you should start yourself from seeds and transplant, others you can direct seed and some should be ordered as plugs. We'll start with the entire list and then break it up so you can see which ones like cool weather and which prefer hot summers. In the next chapter we will cover which varieties do well direct seeded and which prefer to be transplanted. Then we'll talk about harvesting and spacing information more in depth.

Know that there is a lot of repetition between the categories. This is intentional; part of being a flower farmer is knowing just about everything there is to know about varieties and how to grow them. The repetition will help you get the facts down and really start to internalize the information.

My suggestion? Print out these lists and arm yourself with them before you start looking at catalogs.

This is kind of a dumb example, but last year, I became obsessed with a grass called Kiss-Me-Over-the-Garden-Gate (you guys... it's not even that pretty! I have no idea what I was thinking). I had read the GeoSeed description and thought it sounded perfectly lovely. I ordered the seed, but I ran out of time to actually get it planted.

Turns out it's a weed that grows all over my field. I found it growing pretty much everywhere. Did I pick any of it? Nope.

It was (is!) a constant reminder that just because something sounds great in a seed catalog doesn't mean you should buy it.

Varieties to Grow Your First Year

These are all flowers that you can grow and profit from in one season. Some of these flowers are perennials, but they can be grown like annuals. Some need a cool period, and others need heat.

Pretty much all of them are easily grown from seed, although certain varieties are better as plugs. All of the following information on harvesting, spacing and succession planting came from a variety of references and personal experience. These were my go to resources in compiling this information:

- *Specialty Cut Flowers: The Production of Annuals, Perennials, Bulbs, and Woody Plants for Fresh and Dried Cut Flowers* by Allan M. Armitage and Judy Laushman
- Johnnysseeds.com
- Succession Planting: How to Keep the Harvest Going All Season Long by Floret

Cool Flowers

Lisa Mason Ziegler is the expert here! She has revolutionized cut flower growing by helping farmers and gardeners alike produce more flowers and extend our growing season. In her book, _Cool Flowers: How to Grow and Enjoy Long-Blooming Hardy Annuals Using Cool Weather Techniques_, she discusses how to plant flowers in the fall or early spring to get more flowers sooner. I am listing some of the most popular cool flowers, but to get a full list, check out her book.

All of these flowers can be fall or early spring (8-10 weeks before the last frost) planted. Row covers may be needed for additional frost protection but these are hardy little plants who love cooler weather. In fact some plants, like sweet peas, won't grow without it!

Achillea
Varieties: Colorado Mix, Mixed Berries, etc.
Spacing: 12"
Harvesting: flowers are fully formed and pollen is visible

Agrostemma
Varieties: Ocean Pearls, Purple Queen
Spacing: 6"
Number of Plantings: 2-3
Frequency: every 2 weeks
Harvesting: when 1-2 flowers in spray are open

Ammi
Varieties: Graceland, Green Mist

Spacing: 9"
Number of Plantings: 2
Frequency: every 3-4 weeks
Harvesting: 80% of the florets are open

Bells of Ireland
Varieties: Bells of Ireland
Spacing: 12"
Number of Plantings: 2
Frequency: every 3 weeks
Harvesting: when flowers are 1/2 open

Bupleurum
Varieties: Graffiti, Green Gold
SpacingL 8-10"
Number of Plantings: 4
Frequency: every 2 weeks
Harvesting: flower heads show color and are almost all the way open

Campanula
Varieties: Medium, Champion
Spacing: 12"
Harvesting: when 1-2 buds are open, 2-3 for champion

Centaurea
Varieties: Boy Series
Spacing: 6"
Number of Plantings: every 2-3
Frequency: every 3 weeks
Harvesting: flowers are 1/4 - 1/2 open

Cerinthe

Varieties: Kiwi Blue
Spacing: 9-12"
Number of Plantings: 2-3
Frequency: every 3-4 weeks
Harvesting: most stages, when flowers form

Cynoglossum
Varieties: Chinese Forget Me-Not, Rose Magic
Spacing: 9"
Number of Plantings: 2-3
Frequency: every 3-4 weeks
Harvesting: 1/3-1/2 blooms are open

Daucus
Varieties: Dara
Spacing: 12"
Number of Plantings: 2
Frequency: every 3-4 weeks
Harvesting: 80% are open

Delphinium
Varieties: Belladonna, Magic Fountains
Spacing: 9"
Number of Plantings: 1-2
Harvesting: 1/4-1/3 of blooms on the stem are open

Dianthus
Varieties: Amazon, Sweet, (both FYF)
Spacing: 6"
Harvesting: flowers are 10% open

Dill
Varieties: Bouquet, Vierling

Spacing: 12"
Number of Plantings: 2-3
Frequency: every 3-4 weeks
Harvesting: when flowering

Dusty Miller
Varieties: Circadians, New Look
Spacing: 9"
Number of Plantings: 2
Frequency: every 4 weeks
Harvesting: when stems are hard and woody

Godetia (clarkia)
Varieties: Grace Series
Spacing: 4-5" unpinched, 20-24" pinched
Number of Plantings: 3
Frequency: every 3 weeks
Harvesting: when first flowers on the stem are open

Flowering Kale
Varieties: Crane Series, etc.
Spacing: 6"
Harvesting: when flowers are colored and 6"

Lisianthus
Varieties: Arena, Doublini, Echo, Miriachi, etc.
Spacing: 6"
Number of Plantings: 1-2
Harvesting: when one or more flowers on the stem are open; they will not continue to open once cut

Larkspur
Varieties: QIS, Giant Imperial, Messenger

Spacing: 4-6"
Number of Plantings: 3
Frequency: every 3 weeks
Harvesting: when 1/4 to 1/2 of the flowers are open on the stem

Matricaria
Varieties: Magic, Tetra, Ultra
Spacing: 8"
Number of Plantings: 2-3
Frequency: every 3 weeks
Harvesting: when flower cluster is mostly open

Nigella
Varieties: Albion, Cramer's, Miss Jekyll, etc...
Spacing: 6"
Number of Plantings: 3-4
Frequency: every 2 weeks
Harvesting: when buds are fully colored but before petals have separated completely from the center

Orlaya
Varieties: White Finch
Spacing: 9"
Harvesting: when 80% are open

Poppies
Varieties: Champagne Bubbles, Colibri (hummingbird)
Spacing: 6" (9" if perennial)
Number of Plantings: 2
Frequency: every 4 weeks
Harvesting: when buds begin to crack; sear stems with heat

Rudbeckia

Varieties: Prairie Sun, Tribola, Indian Summer
Spacing: 12"
Number of Plantings: 2
Frequency: every 4 weeks
Harvesting: when flowers are all the way open

Scabiosa
Varieties: Pincushion, Stellata (perennial: Fama)
Spacing: 9" (12")
Number of Plantings: 3-4
Frequency: every 3 weeks
Harvesting when the center flower just starts to unfurl

Shiso (Perilla)
Varieties: Britton, Red, Green
Spacing: 12"
Number of Plantings: 3
Frequency: every 3 weeks
Harvesting: when stems are mature

Snapdragon
Varieties: Chantilly, Madam Butterfly, Opus, Rocket
Spacing: 9"
Number of Plantings: 3
Frequency: every 3-4 weeks
Harvesting: 1/3-1/2 blooms are open

Statice
Varieties: Fortress, QIS, Pastel Shades, etc...
Spacing: 9"
Number of Plantings: 3
Frequency: every 3 weeks
Harvesting: when you can see the white of the individual flowers

Stock
Varieties: Cheerful, Katz, Iron
Spacing: 6"
Number of Plantings: 2
Frequency: every 2-3 weeks
Harvesting: when 1/2 the flowers are open on the inflorescence

Sweet Peas
Varieties: Elegance, Spencer, etc.
Spacing: 6-8"
Number of Plantings: 2
Frequency: every 3 weeks
Harvesting: when stems reach 12" and 2-3 flowers start to color

Tender Annuals

These are annuals that love the heat. It is best to plant them out after your last frost date. Note that while I have sunflowers listed here, they are actually somewhat cold tolerant and can be planted under low tunnels 4 weeks before your last spring frost unlike the rest of the summer loving annuals which need the warm temps to survive.

Ageratum
Varieties: Blue Horizon, Tall Blue Planet
Spacing: 9"
Number of Plantings: 2
Frequency: every 4 weeks
Harvesting: spikes 3/4 open

Amaranthus
Varieties: Coral Fountains, Hot Biscuit, Oppeo
Spacing: 12"
Number of Plantings: 2-4
Frequency: every 3 weeks
Harvesting: when 3/4 are open

Artemisia
Varieties: Sweet Annie, Silver King
Spacing: 12"
Harvesting: once flower heads have developed or once stems are green and full

Basil
Varieties: Aromatto, Lemon, Cinnamon, African Blue, Oriental
Spacing: 8"
Number of Plantings:2-3
Frequency: every 3-4 weeks
Harvesting: when flowers begin to open

Celosia
Varieties: Cramer's, Chief, Pampas Plume, etc...
Spacing: 9" (6" for Bombay)
Number of Plantings: 3-4
Frequency: every 2-4 weeks
Harvesting: when flowers along bract are completely open

Cosmos
Varieties: Cupcake, Double Click, Sensation, Versailles
Spacing: 9"
Number of Plantings: 3
Frequency: every 2-4 weeks
Harvesting: when buds begin to crack

Euphorbia
Varieties: Mountain Snow
Spacing: 6-9"
Harvesting: cut before flowers are fully open but when bracts are colored

Gomphrena
Varieties: QIS Series, Strawberry Fields
Spacing: 6-9"
Number of Plantings: 2-3
Frequency: every 3-4 weeks
Harvesting: when flowers are in color and partially open

Marigold
Varieties: Jedi
Spacing: 8"
Number of Plantings: 2-3
Frequency: every 3 weeks
Harvesting: when flowers open

Millet
Varieties: Lime Light, Purple Majesty, etc.
Spacing: 1/2"
Frequency of planting: weekly
Harvesting: when fully open

Sunflowers
Varieties: Pro Cut, Vincent
Spacing: 6"
Frequency of Planting: every 1-2 weeks
Harvesting: when petals begin to lift

Zinnias
Varieties: Benary's Giant, Oklahoma, Persian Carpet, Queen Red Lime
Spacing: 12"
Number of Plantings: 3 - 4
Frequency: every 3 weeks
Harvesting: when stems harden and flower heads no longer flop

Fillers & Greenery

These are the workhorses of your bouquets. They provide the background and base to your arrangements to highlight your focal flowers. Grow LOTS of them, especially the greens. You can never have too much greenery!

Amaranthus
Varieties: Coral Fountains, Hot Biscuit, Oppeo
Spacing: 12"
Number of Plantings: 2-4
Frequency: every 3 weeks
Harvesting: when 3/4 are open

Ammi
Varieties: Graceland, Green Mist
Spacing: 9"
Number of Plantings: 2
Frequency: every 3-4 weeks

Harvesting: 80% of the florets are open

Artemisia
Varieties: Sweet Annie, Silver King
Spacing: 12"
Harvesting: once flower heads have developed or once stems are green and full

Basil
Varieties: Aromatto, Lemon, Cinnamon, African Blue, Oriental
Spacing: 8"
Number of Plantings:2-3
Frequency: every 3-4 weeks
Harvesting: when flowers begin to open

Bells of Ireland
Varieties: Bells of Ireland
Spacing: 12"
Number of Plantings: 2
Frequency: every 3 weeks
Harvesting: when flowers are 1/2 open

Bupleurum
Varieties: Graffiti, Green Gold
SpacingL 8-10"
Number of Plantings: 4
Frequency: every 2 weeks
Harvesting: flower heads show color and are almost all the way open

Cerinthe
Varieties: Kiwi Blue
Spacing: 9-12"

Number of Plantings: 2-3
Frequency: every 3-4 weeks
Harvesting: most stages, when flowers form

Cynoglossum
Varieties: Chinese Forget Me-Not, Rose Magic
Spacing: 9"
Number of Plantings: 2-3
Frequency: every 3-4 weeks
Harvesting: 1/3-1/2 blooms are open

Daucus
Varieties: Dara
Spacing: 12"
Number of Plantings: 2
Frequency: every 3-4 weeks
Harvesting: 80% are open

Dill
Varieties: Bouquet, Vierling
Spacing: 12"
Number of Plantings: 2-3
Frequency: every 3-4 weeks
Harvesting: when flowering

Dusty Miller
Varieties: Circadians, New Look
Spacing: 9"
Number of Plantings: 2
Frequency: every 4 weeks
Harvesting: when stems are hard and woody

Eucalyptus

Varieties: Lemon Bush, Silver Drop, Silver Dollar
Spacing: 12"
Harvesting: after stems mature and leaves feel leathery

Euphorbia
Varieties: Mountain Snow
Spacing: 6-9"
Harvesting: cut before flowers are fully open but when bracts are colored

Millet
Varieties: Lime Light, Purple Majesty, etc.
Spacing: 1/2"
Frequency of planting: weekly
Harvesting: when fully open

Mint
Varieties: Apple, Mountain, Orange, Pineapple, Spearmint
Spacing: 12"
Harvesting: when stems are long enough to use in bouquets

Orlaya
Varieties: White Finch
Spacing: 9"
Harvesting: when 80% are open

Shiso (Perilla)
Varieties: Britton, Red, Green
Spacing: 12"
Number of Plantings: 3
Frequency: every 3 weeks
Harvesting: when stems are mature

Statice
Varieties: Fortress, QIS, Pastel Shades, etc...
Spacing: 9"
Number of Plantings: 3
Frequency: every 3 weeks
Harvesting: when you can see the white of the individual flowers

Perennials

You will notice that the following flowers are also on the cool flower's chart. They are first year flowering and can be grown as single season annuals or overwintered for next year. However, some perennials will develop diseases and produce fewer flowers after 2-3 years, at which point you will need to remove them.

Achillea
Varieties: Colorado Mix, Mixed Berries, etc.
Spacing: 12"
Harvesting: flowers are fully formed and pollen is visible

Delphinium
Varieties: Belladonna, Magic Fountains
Spacing: 9"
Number of Plantings: 1-2
Harvesting: 1/4-1/3 of blooms on the stem are open

Mint

Varieties: Apple, Mountain, Orange, Pineapple, Spearmint
Spacing: 12"
Harvesting: when stems are long enough to use in bouquets

Rudbeckia
Varieties: Prairie Sun, Tribola, Indian Summer
Spacing: 12"
Number of Plantings: 2
Frequency: every 4 weeks
Harvesting: when flowers are all the way open

Scabiosa
Varieties: Pincushion, Stellata (perennial: Fama)
Spacing: 9" (12")
Number of Plantings: 3-4
Frequency: every 3 weeks
Harvesting when the center flower just starts to unfurl

Big Ideas:

- Grow what sells, not just what you like
- Think about all of the different aspects that go into each variety: easy to grow, sells well, long vase life

Get Real: Time to Dig In

1. What flowers have you grown in the past and loved?

2. What are you most excited about growing?

3. What are other flower farmers in your state growing? What aren't they growing? Is there a reason they aren't growing that particular flower?

4. Are there flowers that your florists want but can't find due to quality? You'll have to do some actual leg work here and ask them!

5. Do you want to grow large amounts of specialty crops to sell wholesale or to florists? Or do you want to grow more varieties of flowers in smaller quantities for design work?

6. What will you be the most successful at growing? This should probably be something you've grown before. Is there a need for these flowers in your area?

7. Do you have perennials established in your yard or garden that you can use as cuts? *extra tip: cut everything you can find to test its vase life!

8. What particular difficulties will you face throughout your growing season? Thrips? Drought? Clay soils? Wind?

9. Which flowers will do best in your given climate with your particular difficulties?

6

PLANTING GUIDE

DIRECT SEEDING, TRANSPLANTING, SUCCESSION PLANTING, SPACING
AND PINCHING

This is where it gets real, you guys. You have your list of what you're growing and where you're growing, so let's get to the fun part of actually starting and taking care of those seed babies!

Before You Plant a Single Seed

Remember how I said that almost all of the flowers on the First Year Flowering List are relatively easy to start from seed? I have lisianthus and eucalyptus plants growing on trays right now. However, I also planned ahead and ordered plugs because lisianthus seedlings grow so slowly (remember: just because it's easy to grow from seed doesn't mean you should!).

Not sure what in the world I'm talkin' about? Plugs are baby seedlings that come in different sized trays. You will see flower farmers throw around terms like 128s and 220s and that just means how many plants come in a given tray. The smaller the number, the larger the seedling.

You know how in the last chapter we talked about how good cut flower varieties are more than just pretty? They have to meet certain requirements to make the cut. Seed starting is the same thing. You need to think about ALL the factors that go into each and every variety that you plant:

- How much space you have
- The amount of time it takes before the seedling can be transplanted
- Consistent watering schedule
- Ambient air temperature
- What that particular seed needs to germinate: light or darkness
- The type of growing medium you're using etc...

One of the most important things I've learned so far is that plants will grow, often times without much more than some water and light. But your goal as a flower farmer is not just to get plants to grow, your goal is to get them to thrive. This starts in the seedling stage. You want to start out with the best and healthiest seedlings possible. Just getting them to grow isn't enough. To make a profit you have to excel in providing more than the minimal survival needs for any given flower.

Think of seed starting as being similar to athletics. I can run, but I am no Olympic athlete. To become an Olympian, you need to eat the right foods and train in a certain way. Everything you do comes down to your performance. You want your flowers to put on the performance of a lifetime (quite literally) in order to make the most money.

Ordering Plugs

Plugs are ordered through brokers and the only broker that exclusively sells cut flower plugs is Farmer Bailey. He's a flower farmer himself, which is so great because you know that you're buying the real deal.

Germania and Gloeckner are the two other main sources to buy flower plugs. I go through Germania, mostly because they had an easier sign up process. Both are good.

Whichever broker you go through, you will need a tax I.D. to set up an account, but aside from that it is a simple process. Plants you should order as plugs are listed below, some because they are slow growing or because seeds are not available:

- African Blue Basil
- Eucalyptus
- Lisianthus
- Mint (apple, spearmint, pineapple)

You may want to think about ordering plugs of some of the cool flowers (hardy annuals) as well. They can be grown from seed, but often are tricky to germinate or need a cooling period after germination. If you are already overwhelmed with starting easier seeds, go ahead and order these plugs as well:

- Bells of Ireland
- Delphinium
- Larkspur
- Poppies
- Scabiosa Fama

- Stock

Often you can find these same plants at local greenhouses, however, some are treated with growth regulators so they stay small before being sold or they are the bedding variety of the same plant, which means that their stems will never be tall enough to cut. Be sure to check before you buy, or save yourself the trouble and just order them.

Seed Starting: Growing Station (Rack)

Let's get started with how to make this whole seed starting thing work. The way I see it, if you want to start your own seeds you have three options: use a greenhouse, set up a growing station complete with shelves and fluorescent lights OR use a window sill. Complete honesty? I can't even keep houseplants alive, so the whole light from a windowsill has never worked for me, and I definitely don't have a greenhouse. That leaves me with setting up a growing station. Here's how to do it.

Requirements for a growing station:

- Shelving
- Fluorescent lights (warm and cool)
- Heat mats
- Fan
- 4' shop lights
- Temperature controlled area

Most seeds germinate between 60-70 degrees, and soil is typically 10 degrees cooler than the ambient room temperature.

Here are a couple videos I found to help you see how it all works. This YouTube video, Indoor Grow Light System, does a great job explaining all the things you need. And this video, What's Sprouting, from the Gardener's Workshop Farm is a great little tour of their seed starting setup.

You can find wire shelving at most hardware stores: Lowes, Home Depot, Sam's Club, etc... all have similar products. You will want one that is 4 feet wide, so you don't waste any of the lighting. Shop lights and bulbs are available at any home supply store and even WalMart. I bought basic heat mats from Amazon. You can also DIY heat mats with rope lighting.

Seed Starting: Soil Blocks vs. Flats

The two main methods of sowing seeds are soil blocking or using potting soil in trays. Both have their advantages and disadvantages.

You will see a lot of smaller farms using soil blocks because they are more space efficient and seedlings can be transplanted sooner. Soil blocks are especially great for small seeds. You can fit 240 little seedlings on a single 12 x 16" tray. The seedlings are typically ready to go out in the field within 4-6 weeks.

Flats are great because it's a straightforward process: fill it with dirt. Easy enough. Flats are a standardized size (10x20) and come with a certain number of cells. The smaller the cell size the larger the number of cells in that flat. They're more suited to greenhouse growing but you can try to make it work indoors. Generally you'll want to start with the smallest cells and as the seedlings get bigger "bump them up" into bigger cells.

There are two sizes of soil blockers, ¾" and 2". You can use the mini soil blocker (¾") for all smaller seeds but for bigger seeds like zinnias, sunflowers, and cosmos you'll want to either use the 2" blocker or a 128 cell flat.

Cuttings

Often times you can take cuttings of plants you already have in order to propagate them. This can be done with some of the varieties from Chapter 5, like African Blue Basil or mint (or if you went rogue: dahlias and scented geranium). You have to be careful though because some plants are patented which means that while you can sell that plant (or stems from that plant), you cannot sell new plants (or stems) that come from it.

Direct Sowing

Direct sowing (planting seeds rather than seedlings/plugs in your bed) is often recommended for these varieties:

- Amaranthus

- Ammi
- Bachelor's buttons
- Bells of Ireland
- Bupleurum
- Cosmos
- Larkspur
- Zinnia
- Sunflowers

Direct seeding is again a function of space and time. It saves both resources and your personal time to direct seed. Also, these seeds can result in healthier plants since they don't have to be transplanted. You'll need to keep them wet (water at least 2x a day!) and consider covering the freshly sown seeds with a row cover to keep the pests at bay. As long as it's after your last frost date you don't even need hoops, just lay the row cover (like agribon) on the bed and water like you normally would. Once the seedlings are a few inches tall you can take it off and you'll be all set.

How Much to Plant & Succession Planting

How much to plant of any given flower is a struggle all flower farmers face. In her awesome book, *The Flower Farmer*, Lynn Byczynski says, "The best strategy for a beginning flower grower is to plant many different kinds of flowers in significant quantities. A packet of this and a packet of that just isn't going to work. Be extravagant in your planting - the worst that could happen is that you'll have more flowers than you need and they'll go unharvested. Seeds are relatively cheap, so don't be afraid to plant more than you think you'll need." Yes and yes, no matter how much planning you do you'll never know exactly what it is your market wants until you're selling to them.

That being said, give yourself grace. You don't have to grow everything or grow a lot of any certain flowers. Be your own boss and do what you think you can handle. This year I've given myself permission to not harvest everything. Just because it's growing doesn't mean I have to pick it. Consider this your permission to be less than perfect. Do what you can and do it well.

If you are looking for specific stem counts, *Specialty Cut Flowers* by Allan M. Ermitage and Judy Laushman lists the number of stems per plants for many varieties. It's a good starting point until you have your own records.

In her blog post "Succession Planting: How To Keep the Harvest Going All Season Long" the one and only Erin Benzecain of Floret, categorizes certain varieties as *cut and come again, medium producers,* and *one shot wonders.* This post is super helpful and will help you see how long you can harvest from any single plant.

Harvest length, or the amount any plant produces, goes into how many times any given plant can be planted in that season, ensuring that you don't have any lulls in flower production. The technical term is succession planting and if you go to my "Resources" page on the *Grow Flowers* website I'll send you the complete succession planting guide to get you going!

Mapping Your Field

Before you start planting, you should draw a layout of your field. Use graph paper to draw it to scale, marking each bed's width and length. Write in which plants will go where. Your layout can change as your season progresses, if you run out of space, or have a crop failure, but this will give you a method to follow and you can plan accordingly for bed rotations for the following year.

How to Plant

In his book *The New Organic Grower*, Eliot Coleman writes that there are three concerns when setting out transplants: moisture, soil contact, and consistent depth of setting. Blocks (or plugs) should be wet when setting out and placed firmly in the soil without any air pockets. Tamp the soil around the seedling and irrigate immediately after planting.

Seedlings should be planted deep, all the way up to their bottom leaves (like tomato plants). Spoons, knives, or PVC pipes are excellent hole makers if you don't have a dibbler. If you are planting in plastic mulch, you can easily make holes with your hands. If you are using landscape fabric, pre-burn holes 3" in diameter with either a flame weeder or a hand-held propane torch. Floret has another awesome post called "Growing With Landscape Fabric" if you want to see how it all works.

Pinching

Pinching increases yields of certain flowers. In *The Flower Farmer*, Byczynski says, "When you pinch a plant, it sends out new stems below the spot where you pinched it. By cutting off the growing tip before it has a chance to bloom, you stimulate the plant to branch and send up multiple stems that bloom at the same time. An unpinched snapdragon, as an example, will send up one flower stem. A snapdragon that is pinched will send up multiple flowers. It may seem obvious that you should pinch snaps in order to get more flowers, but not everyone does. That's because there is a trade-off in height and earliness - unpinched snaps are taller and bloom earlier than pinched snaps. Pinching, then, can be a way of extending the bloom time of a specific flower; you can leave some unpinched for an early crop and pinch the rest for later blooms."

The goal with pinching is to get the plant to throw out more shoots from the bottom of the plant. You'll want to pinch when the plant has at least three leaf nodes, simply take off (pinch) the top node and you're good to go. These are the varieties that respond well to pinching:

- Ageratum
- Amaranthus
- Basil
- Bells of Ireland
- Branching sunflowers
- Celosia (all except bombay)
- Cosmos
- Eucalyptus
- Lisianthus
- Marigolds
- Sweet Peas
- Zinnias

Netting

Some crops are especially susceptible to wind and rain and need extra support, which can be provided through netting. Tenax makes a plastic netting called Hortonova that you can buy off of Amazon.

Varieties that need to be netted are as follows: (info from Harris seed chart)

- Ageratum
- Amaranthus
- Ammi
- Bells of Ireland
- Campánula
- Delosia
- Cosmos
- Delphinium
- Dianthus
- Feverfew
- Kale
- Larkspur
- Rudbeckia
- Scabiosa
- Snapdragon
- Statice
- Stock
- Zinnias

All the varieties that need netting are on the "Harris Seeds Cut Flower Quick Facts Growing Guide" - print it out and keep it handy.

Big Ideas:

- Grow what sells, not just what you like
- Think about all of the different aspects that go into each variety: easy to grow, sells well and has a long vase life.

Get Real: Time to Dig In

1. Which is better for your life right now: seed starting or plugs?

2. Do you have time to start your own seeds? Are you good at it? Or will it result in wasted time and money? (NOTE: you'll always lose some seedlings, but I say if you can have a minimum of a 50% success rate it's still worth it!)

3. How much space do you have (realistically) to start seeds?

4. What's the general temperature in your house or seed starting area? Will you need to use heat mats or additional heating?

5. What plants do you have growing already that you could take cuttings from?

6. If you're not great at seed starting, is there a way you can barter something you're good at in exchange for seedlings? If you have other farmers in your area this might be a great way to get some plants!

7. What are you growing that will need to be pinched?

8. What are you growing that will need to be netted?

7

Remember all that real talk in Chapter One about knowing your weaknesses and strengths?

Well, my weakness is that I live in a mental fantasy world where bugs and weeds don't exist and my soil has all the right nutrients for all the right plants.

Yep. I may be a flower-farm-planning ninja but this right here, all this pest and soil management, is my achilles heel.   This is me saying, do what I say, not what I do!

Fertilizing

Plants need more nutrients than are often available in the soil. If you got a soil test done, then you already know what your soil is lacking and can amend with whatever your extension office recommends. However, if you are planning on growing with organic methods, you may need to do a little leg-work to find comparable amendments since most extension offices recommend traditional fertilizers that are not organic.

In addition to compost, you can also encourage leaf and flower development with fish emulsion, kelp, and compost tea. Generally, these are better applied through a sprayer, which you can find at your local hardware store. If you do plan on using compost tea, a quick Google search will bring up a great deal of information and tutorials on how to make your own.

This is also the section where I would bring up cover cropping if I actually knew how to do it. Instead I'll point you to my favorite resources that I keep reading and never understanding.

- Homegrown Humus: Cover Crops in a No-Till Garden by Anna Hess
- Choosing a Spring Cover Crop by Eric Venturini, Education Coordinato, Johnny's Selected Seeds
- Managing Cover Crops Profitably - Sustainable Agriculture and Research Education

Diseases

One of the best ways to combat diseases is by starting with healthy soils. Healthier soils result in fewer diseases (and pests!). Additionally, you can prevent the spread of viruses by pulling out any infected plants immediately. Dispose of them far (far!) away from you plants. Don't add them to your compost pile and make sure you disinfect your tools. You want to keep your plants as healthy as possible.

Here are a couple of articles on diseases you may encounter and how to combat them naturally.

- Rodale's Organic Life - Common Plant Diseases (http://www.rodalesorganiclife.com/garden/common-plant-diseases)
- Organic Grower's School - Organic Disease Control

Pests

Here is a list of a few common flower pests and what you can use to prevent or treat them. Arbico Organics (Arbico Organics) is a great resource for natural products and sprays, but I've also included Amazon links.

Japanese beetles

Japanese beetles are sluggish in the mornings and evenings, and it is actually extremely therapeutic to go through a row of sunflowers picking them off and crushing them on the ground. Another method is to use beetle traps (available here). Some say not to use beetle traps because they actually attract more beetles, but I put them out early to mid-June and found few left on my flowers.

Slugs

Slugs are terrible. We had them in our first garden as newlyweds and I am pretty sure they drove me to tears. Try Sluggo (available here).

Caterpillars

When these first showed up, it was hard for me to think of them as the evil little bugs they really are -- that is until they started chewing through all my stems. They would COVER entire roots of a plant. I was pretty grossed out. Bacillus Thuricide (BT) is an organic spray and your best bet against them. Buy it here.

Gnats

These aren't the worst problem, but they aren't pleasant, and you don't want to give your customer gnat-covered flowers. Gnatrol is an organic option. Buy it here.

Aphids

Oh aphids. You can try spraying them off with a hose, but one of the best bets is to order in some ladybugs to eat all of them.

Grasshoppers

These are my least favorite of all of the above. Last year I would go into mini-rages whenever I found one in my plot. I would stamp on them any chance I could. Now I just lop off their heads. I hate grasshoppers -- and crickets, for that matter. There isn't much you can do outside of applying NOLO Bait (buy here). Make sure you buy and apply it early to get them while they are still young. Otherwise it is not very effective.

In addition to the above products, you should think about having these on hand in case you need them:

- Safer Insceticidal Soap
- PyGanic
- Diatomaceous Earth
- Neem Oil

Animals

Animals can completely ruin a crop or destroy your tuber investments. I was expecting the deer and rabbits, but didn't anticipate all the damage from the cats using my newly plowed field as a litter box! They got into so many different patches, and there was nothing quite as gross as coming across cat poop while planting. Hopefully the following list will save you money - and some disgusting cat poop discoveries.

Here's a list of common animal pests and what can be done about them:

Deer

You need a fence. Thankfully you have options. Liquid fences often work, and are easy to make. To make, mix a gallon of milk with as much hot sauce as you can handle shaking out, and then bring it to a boil for 10 minutes or so. You can add garlic cloves and anything else that will smell sort of rotten (think old cottage cheese or jalapeños). Let it cool and beat in some raw eggs before straining it through cheesecloth or a flour sack towel. Let it sit outside, covered to get nice and warm (and rotten) for a few days before adding it to a sprayer and applying it to the plants. It smells TERRIBLE. But it works. You have to reapply every couple weeks and after heavy rains.

If making nasty soup spray isn't your cup of tea you can try fencing. You want it to be 7-8 ft tall and you can find these just about anywhere, including Amazon. Some people swear by them, and some just swear at them. You choose. Electric fences are supposed to be effective too. You basically run two electric wires around the perimeter of your plot 3 feet away from each other in width and 4 feet or so difference in height. This confuses the deer. They can't understand depth perception and won't jump something they can't understand. To add on to it, the wires will shock them to further abort their attempts. You can even put some corn syrup on aluminum foil attached to the outer electric wire to teach them that it is there.

We actually used fishing wire as a fence. It worked for about half a season, and then I saw deer jump over it. It is a good illusion because you can't tell the fishing wire is there. In fact, I ran into it on numerous occasions. It completely freaked me out.

Rabbits

Rabbits are little munchers. The only thing of mine that they got into was the craspedia which was closest to the timber. I put down some Dried Blood Meal (link), and the smell kept them away. If you have the time and ambition, you could also dig a trench around the perimeter of your plot to install 2-3' wire fencing. Georgia Newberry has a great illustration on how to do this in her book, *The Flower Farmer's Year: How to Grow Cut Flowers for Pleasure and Profit*.

Big Ideas:

- Start with soil fertility
- Keep various insecticides on hand: you'll never know when you need them!
- Expect flower loss due to animals

Get Real: Time to Dig In

1. Make a Soil Action Plan:

  - Get soil tested
  - Decide on what methods you are going to use to build soil quality
  - Make a list of what amendments you need
  - Figure out how to cover crop effectively and then email me and tell me how to do it too.

2. What disease issues have your plants had in the past? What methods worked and what didn't? What will you try next to treat or fix the problem?

3. What types of bugs have you struggled with? What methods worked and what didn't? What will you try next to prevent them?

4. How are you going to proactively prevent loss from both bugs and animals?

5. Shopping List (I've started it, you finish it with what you know you'll need):
• Neem Oil
• Copper Fungicide
• Safer Insecticidal Soap
•
•
•

8

HOW TO KEEP YOUR FLOWERS FRESH

HARVESTING, STORING AND CONDITIONING

f you aren't already overwhelmed with all of the different things it takes to grow a given flower, harvesting and solution information can be what pushes you over the edge. It did for me at least. I seriously considered making laminated index cards with pictures of all the varieties of flowers I was growing along with all relevant culture information that I would need out in the field. The only reason I didn't is because I was too tired from researching all the information.

After a week or two you'll get the hang of it.

Harvesting Tools

There are a few things you will need before you begin harvesting, namely buckets and clippers.

Buckets are easier to come by than it may seem. My buckets are a mix of food grade buckets from Lowe's, grocery store buckets, and plastic trash bins. A lot of times grocery stores or big box stores will dispose of their buckets after big holidays. Trader Joe's always seems to have extras. You can also use small plastic trash bins from big-box stores. I use the plastic trash bins from Ikea, and they are especially sturdy for their price. The Dollar Tree is another good place to look.

For clippers, Falco #5 and ARS clippers are both great options. Fiskers also makes clippers that you can find at most box stores, but I always end up pinching my hands in them and they get dull quickly.

Solutions: Hydrating vs. Holding vs. Preservatives vs. Anti-Ethelyene

The University of North Carolina has partnered with the ASCFG over the last 15 years to conduct trials on the vase life of flowers with different solutions. You can read the original article, "Postharvest Information," by clicking here.

According to their study, "The efficacy of floral preservatives will vary greatly with the water quality and species. Be sure to test preservatives to find the ones that are best for your operation. Always follow mixing directions as floral preservatives can be either ineffective or detrimental if supplied to the flowers in the wrong concentration. Flowers will be damaged if the preservative is too concentrated and the biocide will be too diluted to be effective if the floral preservative concentration is too low."

Makes complete sense.

You guys, I've spent so much time reading all of the info I can find and it's still clear as mud. Here's what I suggest you do:

1. Clean all your buckets super well with bleach.
2. Buy the book *Postharvest Handling of Cut Flowers and Greens A Practical Guide for Commercial Growers,*

Wholesalers, and Retailers and make it your life mission to memorize everything in it (btw sleeping with it under your pillow is NOT effective).

Harvesting Information

Cutting (harvesting flowers) is like an advanced science in and of itself. Some flowers need to be harvested daily while others can stay on the plant a little longer. Sunflowers, bachelor buttons, and cosmos need to be harvested daily to keep on top of them while zinnias are fine leaving on the plant for an extra day or two. Most flowers like to be harvested while it is still cool, especially flowers like basil and cerinthe, while the optimal time to harvest zinnias is actually 4 in the afternoon.

Here is the general process you should follow with all flowers:

1. Bleach all buckets and fill 1/4-1/3 full of water.
2. Harvest in the cool of very early morning or late evening.
3. Use sharp clippers, and disinfect between crops if one is diseased.
4. Condition flowers for several hours after cutting by storing them in the cooler before using in arrangements.

This is a list of sensitive flowers that require different or extra harvesting care:

Cerinthe - Cerinthe needs to be harvested in the early morning when it is cool out. Cut deep in the plant and immediately put into cool water. I would sometimes even have ice in the bucket. I tried out several different methods of keeping it cool. I would boil the stems for 30 seconds. before putting them in a cup of cold water with ice. I would also dunk the whole stem in a kiddie pool and soak it with cold water for half an hour or so to hydrate it. I never had a problem with it as long as I made sure it got some sort of cold treatment.

I always worried about "immediately" searing or boiling the stems. I would practically run inside the minute I finished cutting my cerinthe or poppies. By the end of the season I figured out that immediately meant as soon as possible, rather than instantaneous.

Poppies - For poppies it is easiest to have a propane torch on hand. Floret has an excellent guide here: Icelandic Poppy Primer.

Snow-on-the-mountain - Treat like cerinthe (BUT that being said, I completely forgot I was supposed to boil the stems and have been harvesting it all summer with no problems).

Stage of Harvest

This refers to how open a flower is when you cut it. Each flower has a particular stage that when cut it performs the best and has a maximum vase life. Tricky, huh?

No worries. I've got you covered. You know those charts in Chapter 3 that talked about what to grow? Well they've also got all of the harvest stages listed for each flower. Go to GrowFlowers.org to get the printable list, print it, laminate it, and you'll be good to go!

General Bloom Times

If you are wondering when your flowers will bloom, TheGardenersWorkshop.com has a bloom availability chart available! This is for their farm specifically, so your flowers may bloom at a different time (mine flower about a month later), but it is helpful to get a general idea.

How to Store Flowers

I'll admit, this is a tough one for new flower farmers. Do you invest in a cooler or even a CoolBot in a business if you are not sure you will succeed? You can get by without a cooler, but it is hard to do. Flowers have a limited life after cutting, and without a cooler it vastly shortens the time you have to sell them before they need to be thrown away.

Here are a few ways to store flowers:

Cool basement - This will work in a pinch. They like cool and dark, and it beats storing them in a hot sun room.

Refrigerator - I found a free refrigerator on Facebook, and it made a huge difference. If you use a refrigerator, you will want to check for any extra cold spots that could freeze your flowers and destroy them. Space is also limited, so while it is not the best solution, it is definitely better than not having anything.

CoolBot cooler - This is what I am doing this year. A CoolBot turns a window A/C into a functioning cooler in an insulated room. It is cheaper than buying a new floral cooler. They have a complete guide, Floral Cooler, on how to set it up.

Floral Cooler- A used floral cooler is an excellent choice if you can find one. Craigslist or Facebook swap sites sometimes have great deals on these.

Renting space - See if any local florists will let you "rent" space in their cooler. This is what one of my local florists does for me and it's awesome. It can be somewhat inconvenient to use someone else's space, but oh-so-worth- it to give you a greater window of time to sell your flowers.

———

Big Ideas:

- Buy good clippers
- Keep everything clean with bleach
- Harvest well, learn which flowers need what
- Condition flowers before using

- Store flowers in a cooler

Get Real: Time to Dig In

1. What kind of clippers are you using? Do you need to get new ones?

2. Do you have lots of buckets already? Or a plan on where to get more?

3. List the supplies you already have here:

4. List the supplies you know you'll need to buy here:

5. Since harvesting will require you to work early mornings and evenings, you might need to reassess your schedule. Write out what changes you will need to make to your daily schedule during harvest season to harvest at the optimal times.

6. How are you going to store your flowers and keep them cool?

9

ARRANGING AND SELLING

This chapter could have an entire book written about it. Instead I'm going to keep it brief and go over the basics on where you can learn all about arranging and selling your flowers. We will cover:

- Learning how to arrange flowers
- Pricing
- Keeping track of sales
- Establishing a brand
- Mastering social media

Learning How to Arrange

Arranging with locally grown flowers comes down to a few key issues: the right ingredients, the right colors, and the right shape/style. As is the case with most things, these elements are affected by your market AND your community's sense of style.

The different types of flowers are:

- Focal or Form: peonies, dahlia, zinnias, etc.
- Spike or Line: snapdragons, larkspur, delphinium, plume celosia, etc.
- Disk: cosmos, marigolds, dianthus, etc.
- Filler or Foliage: basil, mints, etc.

- Air or Texture: grasses, ammi, forget-me-nots, scabiosa

Basically it's a complicated mess and you use what you have and make the best of it. You won't always have the "right" ingredients but you can still make beautiful arrangements.

The best way I've found to start arranging is to use color as a filter. Arielle Chezar is an amazing florist and author (I may be just a BIT of a fangirl) and she's guided my thoughts on this.

In her book, *The Flower Workshop,* she says, "As a rule, it's best to design with one or two main colors in mind. You may feel a spring day calls for sunny yellows or peaches, and an evening dinner begs for purples and blues. Or perhaps the season demands peonies, a flower that almost defines early summer. I have often let one perfect blossom decide my color direction.

Either way, color is your first control. When you have chosen that, you can focus without distraction on flower selection, building on a variety of tones, textures, and shapes until the arrangement has many layers and striking depth.

How do you choose your color pairings? You can opt for analogous shades, those located close together on the color wheel: purples and blues for example, or reds and pinks. Or you can choose to riff on opposite shades, for example, the striking way that burgundy blossoms contrast with pale yellow.

The selective use of color gives you great freedom with flower forms. You can play with shapes, combining a buxom peony, a round ranunculus, and a slender lily in the same arrangement as long as they echo a similar shade and tone. Ultimately, you are attempting to instill a sense of movement in your designs with color, shape and texture. Each arrangement draws the eye through the subtle shifts of color, creating an engaging and compelling effect."

I'm learning that the true art behind floral design is more than the right ingredients or style - anyone can order in flowers and copy a picture. True art is using what is available to you at any given time and turning it into something magical. And that's what's so awesome about us flower farmers and florists who use locally grown flowers exclusively. We're changing how the world sees flowers. People are beginning to understand that beauty can't be standardized, there's no one-fit-all to flower arranging and there shouldn't be.

I'm in Iowa and we get all the latest trends years (YEARS) after they initially come into play in larger metropolitan areas. Add on to that fact that Pinterest has completely revolutionized (read: standardized) the floral business. I know it's tempting to just do what's popular, or what you've always done, but change is the future. Your bouquets don't need to follow a recipe, they need to be beautiful and fresh and reflect the beauty that is all around us.

Resources:

Floret Flowers is an amazing resource in this area. Floret's mastermind, Erin, wrote a blog post titled "Making Market Bouquets" about different market bouquet ingredients throughout the seasons, and her book, The *Cut Flower Garden*, is chock full of inspiration.

Team Flower has lots of designing videos and is even offering a course on how to grow flowers for a summer wedding. You can find their free videos here, but their paid courses are worth every penny! I am going through the "Bouquets and Personnels" course, and it is giving me a lot more confidence in my design work.

The Floral Design Institute (FDI) offers Floral Design Certification with both in-person and online courses. And, they have a YouTube channel full of videos teaching you the principals of design. Watch them here. They are so great and have helped me tremendously.

The *American Society of Specialty Cut Flower Growers* (ASCFG) also has recordings of presentations given by designers throughout the years. It is an excellent resource, especially because it is designed specifically for flower farmers.

Pricing

Flowers are typically sold by the bunch. A bunch can be 5 stems or can vary in size, but most often it is 10 stems.

Pricing differs greatly across the nation. To get a good idea of a competitive market value in your region, sign up for a wholesale account at your local floral wholesalers. This will give you an idea of what the florists in your area are accustomed to paying. The ASCFG also has a chart that states the average amount farmers are making on each variety. You can also check out the Boston market pricing here.

Generally you will make more per stem from farmer's markets than by selling to florists, but you will have to account for the amount of time you spend arranging too.

One more note: Don't be afraid to charge for your flowers. You are providing a quality product.

Alison Ellis is an amazing florist and the creator of the website, Real Flower Business . Her goal is to help florists know exactly what to charge and how to run a successful business. Definitely go check out her site! She has tons of proposals, contracts, workflows, etc. I bought a few of her downloads and really want to take her course, Flower Math. The Florist's Guide to Pricing and Profitability.

Social Media & Website

In today's world, you need a website to reach potential customers. Facebook and Instagram are also instrumental in attracting clients. The best option is to hire a graphic designer who also knows web design and have them build you an entire platform for your farm that could include a logo and brand style. However, the cost of that can add up, so here are some of the best tools to help you create your own websites, logos, and Facebook cover images:

- Squarespace - Squarespace is wonderful for your website because it has modern designs and an easy interface to use. There is also an option to sell products through your website. It does cost money, but in my opinion it is worth it, because it creates such a great design aesthetic.
- Canva - Canva has pre-made logos and marketing templates. It is easy to use and helpful.
- Wordpress - Wordpress is another classic for building your website, but it is not quite as user friendly as the above options.

Big Ideas:

- Use color to start all of your designs
- Price according to your area
- Use social media to your advantage

Get Real: Time to Dig In

1. Is arranging and designing with flowers one of your strengths? Or is it a weakness?

2. What colors are you naturally drawn to?

3. Are there flowers that you know fit your design aesthetic and are easy to grow? List them here:

4. What are the trends both in style and color in your area?

5. Which arranging videos do you have on your to-watch list? Write them down here so you don't forget!

6. What are the general and accepted prices in your area for flowers?

7. How are you going to make your website? Which websites do you find inspiring?

Made in the USA
Middletown, DE
15 December 2024

67147090R00068